Selected Poems of Albert Steffen

For Joy
with love
Daisy Aldan
1968
May

TRANSLATED FROM GERMAN
By DAISY ALDAN

FOLDER EDITIONS — NEW YORK

ACKNOWLEDGMENTS

The translator extends grateful acknowledgment to ILI HACKLÄNDER without whose collaboration these translations could not have existed.

Further gratitude is due to DORA BAKER for invaluable suggestions. Thanks are also extended to Elly Havas Simons, Marlis Schwieger, Ben Clemens, and Kirsten Beata Kux.

Library of Congress Catalog Card Number 68-23771

Distributor: Folder Editions
325 East 57 Street, New York City 10022

NOTE: *The publication of this book has been authorized by the Albert Steffen Foundation.*
Written permission from the translator is required for re-printing of the translations in any form, and for use in commercial recitation.

CONTENTS

Ich tret aus der finsteren Stadt . . .

Ich tret aus der finsteren Stadt
auf das rötlich dampfende Feld
zum bläulich schäumenden Fluss
und will mich baden
vom Staube der Strassen.
Und wie ich schimmernd den Fluten entsteige,
schwebt eine Wolke
von goldenen Bienen heran
und hängt sich wie ein Flügelfell
um meine Schultern.
Und vor mir steht ein Engel,
der kam auf silbernen Sohlen
herübergewandelt und spricht:
"Habe nicht Angst. Sie stechen nicht.
Sie bringen Honig-Botschaft
vom Blütenbaum des Paradieses."

CONTENTS

Schwer ist es, das Schöne zu lassen . . .

Hard is it to abandon the beautiful,
that in movements
ascends,
in faces and trees and flowers
leaning over
from a golden past;
in tones also, in which stars radiate,
and words, borne by Gods,
and Angels, who enfold us,
bestowing the sweetness of brotherly kisses upon the soul.

But other Beings tarry in arid woods;
fruit oozes no juices
to quench their thirst.

And the rolling drums of death across the field there
gather spectres
around the decay.
And I near the Dead,
with the pictures of life,
have the power,
to deliver up hell to itself.
And cannot dispel my pains,
and must endure them
until the end of time.

For sweat runs always
down from the brows of the dying,
and my soul is unworthy,
to be more than a shroud,
to wipe it away.

Guide Mankind,
so rings the promise,
to the Tree of Life,
where the Redeemer bides.
You do it,
by giving away
the Pictures of Paradise.

Warum hat nicht Kraft, uns zu vereinigen . . .

Warum hat nicht Kraft, uns zu vereinigen,
was Ewiges ist
in Baum und Wolke und Licht?
Wir lieben es doch,
wir nehmen es doch in unsere Liebe auf
und hüten es als Treue,
Treue ist doch in Baum und Wolke und Licht
und auch in uns Liebenden.
Warum hat immer wieder das Tier, der Tyrann und der Tod Befugnis,
zu kränken, zu trennen und zu vernichten?

Ach, ist das Grab des Erlösers noch nicht geöffnet,
oder vertrauen wir ihm nicht ganz?

Ob die Liebe kommt in Baum und Wolke und Licht
oder als Auferstandener,
ob du das Antlitz des Menschen oder des Engels hast,
du bist doch immer um mich.
Verwandlung ist auch von Christus geschickt.
Wir müssen in viele Geistergesellschaften treten.
Das Geschick will es hindern.
Doch der Tod schafft die Bahn,
der Tod ist auch von Christus geschickt.

Sieh in dem Baume das Antlitz des Engels,
der in dir wohnt,
das ist, weil das Kreuz wieder grünt,
nicht Baum der Erkenntnis,
nicht Baum des Lebens,
nicht Baum des Sterbens,
nur Baum der Liebe:
Er blüht im Tod und im Leben,
und seine Früchte hängen immer über uns.

Wie die Wolke ins Blau des Himmels hereinrollt:
O Opfer, in der Frommheit erbrausend,
die Dürre wird fruchtbar durch dich.
Aber die Erde ist voller Stätten, wo Mord ist,
Mord, das ist es, was ich wegbringen will.
Dies ward uns Jüngern ja aufgegeben.
Weniger wichtig ist es zu sterben
als Leben zu geben.
Und der Mörder will auch erlösen,
aber zum Nichts.

Baum der Liebe, du leuchtest,
ich schau in dir das Licht des Erlösers,
denn ich sterbe in Christo
und werde vom heiligen Geiste wieder geboren.

Vom blauen Tagesstrahl erstarrt . . .

From the azure ray of day benumbed,
stark and cold
and scarcely mellowed
by the reddish clouds of evening
to tears of parting,
pallid and blind,
gliding across into naught . . .

— — — — — — — — —

Shadows of the dead Moon
hurl
the funeral shrouds . . .

— — — — — — — — —

Yes, cover me wholly
that I endure, that I may bear . . .

— — — — — — — — —

How you nestle
and flatter as down!
I lie embedded
with my head
against your heart:
Angel of the All,
who with your wings,
enfold birth and death
and I listen to the breath
in your bosom . . .

Schwer ist es, das Schöne zu lassen . . .

Schwer ist es das Schöne zu lassen,
das in Bewegungen
aufsteigt,
und Gesichtern und Bäumen und Blumen,
die sich herbiegen
aus goldener Vorzeit,
auch Tönen, in denen noch Sterne erstrahlen,
und Worten, Götter-getragen,
und Engeln, die uns umarmen,
geschwisterlichen Kusses Süsse der Seele schenkend.

Aber andere Wesen weilen in dorrendem Walde,
es tropft nicht die Frucht,
sie zu tränken.

Und des Todes Trommelwirbel über das Feld hin
sammelt Gespenster
bei der Verwesung.
Und ich bei den Toten,
mit den Bildern des Lebens,
habe die Macht,
die Hölle zu übergeben sich selber.
Und weiss nicht die Schmerzen zu scheuchen
und muss sie tragen
bis ans Ende der Welt.

Denn der Schweiss rinnt immer
von der Stirne der Sterbenden,
und meine Seele ist unwert,
mehr als ein Laken zu sein,
ihn wegzuwischen.

Führe die Menschen,
so heisst die Verkündung,
zum Baume des Lebens,
wo der Erlöser harrt.
Du tust es,
wenn du die Bilder
der Paradiese verschenkst.

Schwer ist es, das Schöne zu lassen . . .

Hard is it to abandon the beautiful,
that in movements
ascends,
in faces and trees and flowers
leaning over
from a golden past;
in tones also, in which stars radiate,
and words, borne by Gods,
and Angels, who enfold us,
bestowing the sweetness of brotherly kisses upon the soul.

But other Beings tarry in arid woods;
fruit oozes no juices
to quench their thirst.

And the rolling drums of death across the field there
gather spectres
around the decay.
And I near the Dead,
with the pictures of life,
have the power,
to deliver up hell to itself.
And cannot dispel my pains,
and must endure them
until the end of time.

For sweat runs always
down from the brows of the dying,
and my soul is unworthy,
to be more than a shroud,
to wipe it away.

Guide Mankind,
so rings the promise,
to the Tree of Life,
where the Redeemer bides.
You do it,
by giving away
the Pictures of Paradise.

Warum hat nicht Kraft, uns zu vereinigen ...

Warum hat nicht Kraft, uns zu vereinigen,
was Ewiges ist
in Baum und Wolke und Licht?
Wir lieben es doch,
wir nehmen es doch in unsere Liebe auf
und hüten es als Treue,
Treue ist doch in Baum und Wolke und Licht
und auch in uns Liebenden.
Warum hat immer wieder das Tier, der Tyrann und der Tod Befugnis,
zu kränken, zu trennen und zu vernichten?

Ach, ist das Grab des Erlösers noch nicht geöffnet,
oder vertrauen wir ihm nicht ganz?

Ob die Liebe kommt in Baum und Wolke und Licht
oder als Auferstandener,
ob du das Antlitz des Menschen oder des Engels hast,
du bist doch immer um mich.
Verwandlung ist auch von Christus geschickt.
Wir müssen in viele Geistergesellschaften treten.
Das Geschick will es hindern.
Doch der Tod schafft die Bahn,
der Tod ist auch von Christus geschickt.

Sieh in dem Baume das Antlitz des Engels,
der in dir wohnt,
das ist, weil das Kreuz wieder grünt,
nicht Baum der Erkenntnis,
nicht Baum des Lebens,
nicht Baum des Sterbens,
nur Baum der Liebe:
Er blüht im Tod und im Leben,
und seine Früchte hängen immer über uns.

Wie die Wolke ins Blau des Himmels hereinrollt:
O Opfer, in der Frommheit erbrausend,
die Dürre wird fruchtbar durch dich.
Aber die Erde ist voller Stätten, wo Mord ist,
Mord, das ist es, was ich wegbringen will.
Dies ward uns Jüngern ja aufgegeben.
Weniger wichtig ist es zu sterben
als Leben zu geben.
Und der Mörder will auch erlösen,
aber zum Nichts.

Baum der Liebe, du leuchtest,
ich schau in dir das Licht des Erlösers,
denn ich sterbe in Christo
und werde vom heiligen Geiste wieder geboren.

Warum hat nicht Kraft, uns zu vereinigen . . .

Why has not strength to unite us,
what is eternal
in tree and cloud and light ?
surely we love it,
and we receive it into our love
guard it in faithfulness:
Faithful indeed are tree and cloud and light
and also we who love.
Why have always anew the beast, the tyrant and death dominion,
to afflict, to sever and to destroy?

Ah, has the grave of the Saviour not yet been opened,
or do we not have faith in Him wholly?

Whether love comes in tree and cloud and light
or as the Risen One,
whether you bear Man's features or those of an Angel,
you yet encompass me always.
Transformation is also sent by the Christ.
We must join the assemblies of many spiritual Beings.
Fate tries to hinder us.
Yet death fashions the path;
death is also sent by the Christ.

See in the tree the face of the Angel,
who dwells in you,
because the Cross again grows green,
not Tree of Knowledge,
not Tree of Life,
not Tree of Death,
but Tree of Love:
It blooms in death and in life,
and its fruits are ever suspended above us.

As the cloud rolls into the blue of heaven:
O offering, in devotion resounding,
the desert grows fruitful through you.
But the earth is full of sites where murder exists;
murder, that is what I wish to expel.
This was assigned to us disciples.
Less essential is it to die
than to give life.
And the murderer's will is also to save,
but to naught.

Tree of Love, you shine,
I see in you the Redeemer's light,
for I die in Christ
and shall be born again through the Holy Ghost.

Ich ruhte . . .

Ich ruhte,
nicht erfüllt von Geistes Heiterkeit,
traurig gestimmt ob meinem Geschick.
Da rollte
schwarzes Gewölk in die Bläue des Himmels.
Nah gekommen zerfiel es in Dämonen,
grausig gegliedert.
Vom Anprall des ersten Getieres
erlitt ich Schaden.
Es wankten die Knie.
Ich lag und streckte die Hände vor mich
im Kreuze.
Siehe, jetzt fielen die andern Gebilde
in nichts zusammen.
Denn kein Geist
ging durch das Kreuz
ausser Christus.
— Alle Gewitter der Höllen verziehen sich.

Ich ruhte . . .

I rested,
not filled with Spirit-serenity,
in sombre mood over my fate.
There rolled
a black cloud in the blue of the sky.
As it drew near it split into demons,
gruesomely jointed.
From the impact of the first beast
I suffered harm.
My knees gave way.
I lay and extended my hands before me
in the form of a Cross.
See, now the other figures
collapsed to naught.
For no Spirit-being
passed through the Cross
save Christ.
— All the thunder and lightning of hell withdraw.

Eine Windmühle sah ich . . .

Eine Windmühle sah ich
auf dem Gipfel des Hügels.
Sie mahlte den Weizen des Abhangs.
Ich sah sie emporgehoben gen Himmel
und niedersausend zur Erde
durch die Gewalt des Sturmes.
Und die Glut, die er brachte, versengte die Felder
und entblösste den Felsen,
und der Felsen war aus Totengebein.
Aber die Mühle wurde ein Vogel
und schlug mit den Flügeln
furchtbar auf meine Brust.
Und da ich den Vogel mit den Armen umfasste,
sprach er:
Ich komme von dorther,
wo Seelen brennen,
und hole Nahrung dem Feuer.
Denn hier ist Spreu.
Und lange schon mahlt die Mühle leer.
Ehemals sass ich auf dem Balken des Kreuzes dessen, der sagt:
Ich bin das Brot des Lebens.
Höre dies Wort,
Denn ER ist nah deinem Geist . . .

Eine Windmühle sah ich . . .

A windmill I saw
on the top of the hill.
It ground the wheat of the slope.
I saw it uplifted toward heaven
and in rushing descent to the earth
through the tempest's fury.
The smouldering heat in its wake, singed all the fields
and the rock was laid bare,
and the rock was of bones of the dead.
But the mill became a bird
and beat with its wings
fearfully upon my breast.
And as I enfolded the bird in my arms,
it spoke:
I come from yonder,
where souls are burning,
and fetch food for the fire.
For here is chaff.
And long already the mill grinds empty.
Once I was sitting on the beam of the Cross of Him, who says:
I am the Bread of Life.
Receive this Word.
For HE is near your Spirit . . .

Für Rudolf Steiner

Wohl ist die Erde zum Leib des Erlösers geworden,
seit ihn die Kluft verschlungen,
die bis ins Innerste geht,
wo ehemals das Tier des Abgrunds gelauert . . .

Wohl hat es die Höhlung verlassen
und kreist
dem Tode verfallen . . .

Aber die Menschen nähren es noch
mit eigenem Blute.
Und der Leib des Erlösers liegt schlafend,
weil die Menschheit noch träumt in Mord.

Und der Auferstandene
wandelt im All
und spricht mit Jahve:
— "Du richtest!
Aber wer findet die Richtung
im toten Scheine des Mondes?"

Und der Vater erwidert:
"Gerichtete!
Deshalb erlöse sie nicht!
Bleibe bei mir!
Siehe, noch immer verwüsten sie dir den wehrlos schlafenden Leib."

Aber der Sohn, er neigt sich zur Erde!

Für Rudolf Steiner

The earth has indeed been transmuted to the Body of the Redeemer,
since the cleft devoured Him,
which descends to the innermost depths,
where the Beast of the Abyss once lowered . . .

It has indeed forsaken the hollow
and circles
death-dominated . . .

But Men still nourish it
with their own blood.
And the Redeemer's Body lies sleeping,
for Mankind still dreams in murder.

And the Risen One
wanders in the All
and speaks with Jahve:
— "You judge!
But who finds the direction
in the dead light of the moon?"

And the Father replies:
"The condemned!
Therefore redeem them not!
Remain with me!
See, even now they lay waste your defenseless sleeping body."

Still, the Son, He bends down to the earth!

Es schwebte hoch über mir . . .

Es schwebte hoch über mir
im lichtentfremdeten Raume
ein finsterer Adler,
nicht freien Fluges!
— Aber von wem gelenkt?
Sein Kreisen schrieb ein Wort meines Schicksals,
aber es liess keine Spur in der schwarzen Nacht . . .

Die Schwingen rauschten
schwerer vom Dunkel.
Und jählings stürzt' er,
begrub sich in rote Erde hinein.
Ja! Sie war fruchtbar,
aber nicht mehr die Scholle der Kindheit.
Oftmals hab' ich solch keimeschwangeres Ackerland
auf meiner Pilgerfahrt gesehen.
Immer war es einem Gotteshause nah.
Doch hier beim Grabe des Adlers
fand ich das herrlichste Heiligtum.

Ich trat hinein,
An ungeheurer Wölbung sah ich Bilderzüge:
Christus getragen von den Schultern zweier Knaben.
In seinen Händen
gepresst an das Herz
eine Taube.
Die Sonne über ihm.
Fort ging er von Jehovah,
der den Mond zu Häupten hat.

— — — — — — — — — — —

— Das war aus Farben, die noch aufbewahrt
vom Evangelium . . .

Es schwebte hoch über mir . . .

High above me hovered
in light-estranged space
a sombre eagle,
with fettered flight!
— But guided by whom?
His circling spelled a Word of my destiny,
but it left no trace in the black night . . .

Rustling the wings,
weightier from gloom!
He suddenly plunged,
buried himself within the red earth.
Yes, she was fruitful,
but no longer the clod of childhood.
Often in my pilgrimage
have I seen such a seed-pregnant field.
It was always near a House of God.
Yet here by the grave of the eagle
I found the most glorious sanctuary.

I entered in.
On enormous vaultings I saw trains of images:
Christ borne on the shoulders of two youths.
In His hands
pressed to His heart
a Dove.
The Sun above Him.
He strode forth from Jehovah,
whose head the Moon haloes

— — — — — — — — — —

— This was in colors which were still preserved
in the Evangel . . .

Der Jünger sann . . .

Der Jünger sann:
Sei stille, mein Herz,
wenn du Dieses verkündest,
und so wie das Meer,
worauf der Lehrer stand:
Es wogte,
aber es war vom Weltall gehalten.

Tief beugte sich der Lehrer auf die Wellen,
o sieh: Sein Leib,
es war ein Kreuz, von Engeln getragen.

Dann stieg er ans Ufer
und legte die Arme um meinen Hals,
damit mir das Wort
der herrlichen Lehre
werde gegeben.

In seinem Antlitz aber sah ich
Golgatha
sich widerspiegeln.

Der Jünger sann ...

The disciple mused:
Be still, my heart,
when you proclaim This,
and as the sea,
on which the Teacher stood:
It heaved,
but it was sustained by the Cosmos.

Low leaned the Teacher on the waves;
O see: His Body;
it was a Cross, borne by Angels.

Then he stepped ashore
and placed His arms about my neck,
so that the Word
of the glorious Teaching
be given to me.

But in his countenance I saw
Golgotha
reflecting.

Gedanken, scharf und schneidend gehaun . . .

Gedanken, scharf und schneidend gehaun,
die Schwärze zum Spiegel geglättet,
seitlich und senkrecht gekantet ,
als Kreuz auf die Sphäre der Erde gestellt
unter die Wesen der Welt,
die vergehen, —
das ist die Tat meines Leibes: Der Tod.
— Blumen wachsen und welken
auf totem Gestein,
weisser Kelche verhauchender Atem,
blauer Glocken verstummender Ton,
roter Sterne verlöschender Strahl
bringen das Leben
nie mehr zur Wiedergeburt,
und der goldene Vogel in bläulicher Luft,
das Lichtall durchfahrend,
verbrennt.
— Aber seine Asche zerstiebt
und nährt immerdar Gleiches.
Ewig verzehren feurige Tiere sich selbst.
Ach, der einsame Mensch denkt nur das Kreuz.
Doch ein Gott kam herab
zu tragen die tödliche Last.
Ausser mir schleppt er das Kreuz.
In mich komme!
Verwandle das Kreuz der Erkenntnis
zum Baume der Liebe!
O Christus.
Dann kehrt der Phönix als Taube zurück.

Gedanken, scharf und schneidend gehaun . . .

Thoughts hewn so sharply, that they cut,
the blackness smoothed down to a mirror,
sidewise and vertical angled,
as Cross placed on the sphere of the earth
among the beings of the world,
who dissolve, —
that is the deed of my body: Death.
— Flowers wax and wane
upon the dead rock,
white calyxes breathing out life,
blue bells with their muted tone,
red stars with their vanishing rays
bring life
nevermore to rebirth,
and the golden bird in the azure air,
traversing the light-realm
burns.
— But his ashes scatter
and feed what is ever the same.
Fiery beasts forever devour each other.
O, the lonely man's thought is only the Cross.
Yet a God descended
to bear the deadly burden.
Outside me, He drags the Cross.
Into me, come!
Transform the Cross of Knowledge
into the Tree of Love!
O Christ.
Then the Phoenix returns as Dove.

Das All ins Nichts entschwindend über dem Haupte

Das All ins Nichts entschwindend über dem Haupte,
den finstern Alp auf der Brust,
die Füsse niedergezogen von Ketten,
woran die Erdkugel hängt:
stehst du starr
und denkst:
Jetzt geht ein Riss durch das Haus
vom Dach bis zum Keller.
"Fliehn kann ich nimmer!"

Plötzlich schwebt die Seele davon.
Ein himmlischer Hauch
hebt sie zur Gartenhecke.
Verwehtem Falter gleich
hängt sie am Saum einer Sonnenblume.

Aber ein Dämon,
gehüllt in den Staub der zerborstenen Hütte,
folgt ihr,
schwingt eine Schaufel zum Schlag.
Bleibe getrost
Schon senkt sich von oben ein Engel hernieder
und sendet, siehe! den goldenen Pfeil
auf den Feind.

Das All ins Nichts entschwindend über dem Haupte

The All dissolving into void above my head,
the sombre nightmare on my breast,
my feet drawn down by chains,
on which the earth-sphere hangs:
you stand stark
and think:
Now a split cleaves the house
from roof to cellar.
"Never can I flee!"

All of a sudden the soul glides away.
A heavenly breath
lifts her to the garden hedge.
Like a blown butterfly
she dangles on a sunflower's seam.

But a demon,
enveloped in the dust of the shattered hut,
pursues her,
swings a spade for the blow.
Take heart!
An Angel is soaring down from above
and aims, oh see! the golden arrow
at the fiend.

Ja! Er ist auferstanden ...

Ja! Er ist auferstanden,
und das Grab hat er mit sich genommen
und aufgebaut
aus den Steinen die heilige Stadt!
— Und so wollen auch wir
schultern die Särge,
die wir auf Erden bewohnten,
und weiter wandern,
bis wir die Stätte erreichen,
die uns bestimmt ist.
Eines wissen wir ja:
Immer näher werden wir kommen
den Türmen des Himmels
und finden den Ort,
zu errichten das eigene Haus.
Dann hängen
über unseren Häuptern die Sterne
und spenden Helle
dem gastlichen Tische.
Denn wir sind treu;
als Treue aber dürfen wir auch
die Treuen speisen und tränken.

Ja! Er ist auferstanden . . .

Yes! He is risen,
and the grave has He taken with Him
and built up
out of the stones the Sacred City!
— And so we also wish
to shoulder the coffins,
we dwelt in on Earth,
and to wander further,
until we attain the site,
which is destined for us.
One thing we do know:
Always nearer we shall approach
the towers of heaven
and find the place
on which to erect our dwelling.
Then will hover
above our heads the Stars,
and they stream radiance
on the offering Table.
For we are true;
as faithful, however, we also may
give food and drink to the true.

Ichheit schwebt über mir . . .

Ichheit schwebt über mir,
dem irdischen Pilger,
als himmlischer Engel.
Pilger, du musst!
Engel, du willst!
Betet der Pilger,
so schultert der Engel das Lamm.
Schreit der Pilger,
so bändigt der Engel den Stier.
Stockt dem Pilger das Herz,
so reitet der Engel den Löwen.
Löscht dem Pilger das Auge,
so sinkt auf den Engel der Adler.
Ist der Pilger in Frieden entschlafen,
so hat der Engel die Jungfrau gefunden.
Ich-Pilger muss sterben.
Ich-Engel sammle die Geister,
die meinen Leichnam zur Grube getragen.
Sie folgen mir nach
und stellen sich auf
in herrlichen Reigen.
Sie werden Zeichen
am Himmelsgewölbe,
gesprochen von Göttern.
Die Sprache formt Schicksal,
gemäss den Lauten,
streng oder milde.
Nähe oder Ferne vom ewigen Urwort
bestimmt meine Freiheit und Not.

Ichheit schwebt über mir . . .

Selfhood planes over me,
the earthly Pilgrim,
as heavenly Angel.
Pilgrim, you must!
Angel, you will!
When the Pilgrim prays
the Angel shoulders the Lamb.
When the Pilgrim cries,
the Angel bridles the Bull.
When the heart of the Pilgrim flags,
the Angel rides on the Lion.
When the eye of the Pilgrim darkens,
descends on the Angel the Eagle.
When the Pilgrim dies in peace,
then the Angel has found the Virgin.
I-Pilgrim must die.
I-Angel gather the Spirit-beings,
who bore my lifeless body to the grave.
They follow me
and range themselves round
in glorious dances.
They become signs
on the heavenly vaults,
spoken by Gods.
The language forms destiny,
conforming to sounds,
harsh or mellow.
Nearness or distance from the primeval Word
determines my freedom and need.

Was Einer, in tiefe Herzensruhe versunken . . .

Was Einer, in tiefe Herzensruhe versunken,
nach langem Wandern über die Erde hin,
Furcht und Lockung bekämpfend,
mit hellen Sinnen die Welt betrachtend,
in Selbst-Besinnung
errungen hat—:
Laut soll es werden,
als Wort erklingen,
von der Gemeinschaft getragen
die Menschheit wecken.

Was fand der Wandrer
wiederkehrend aus Himmelsräumen
im Zeitgeschehen?
— Heimatlosigkeit.

Schauend von hohem Berge
erfüllt ihn Sehnsucht,
ein Hunger, ungeheuer, nach Erlösung,
höhlt ihn aus,
und seine Augen, einsaugend die Bläue
des Himmels,
einwärts gewandt,
verzehren das Herz.
Er fragt nach Wegen.
Weisung der Menschen führet ihn irre.
Die Linie des Horizontes, voll Verheissung, lügt.
Der hingedehnte Rand verdeckt die Kante
seines Sarges.
Die Erde ist das Grab der Menschheit.

In solcher Finsternis erschien der Lehrer
und hob mit lichter Hand die dunkle Decke.
Der Wandrer schaute in bestimmter Ordnung
Stern an Stern.
Verbunden einer mit dem andern wurden sie
ein Haupt
mit Armen, nach vorne voller Liebe ausgestreckt,
hielten ihn, da schon das Leben ihm entwich
und die Gelenke sich lösten,
stellten ihn aufrecht in Stapfen,
die waren tief in den Boden gehauen.
Der Wandrer aber wusste:
Das waren Tritte seines Geschickes,
ihm vorgegraben für künftige Zeiten,
den Raum umschreibend, der abzuschreiten.

Was Einer, in tiefe Herzensruhe versunken ...

What one, sunk deep in heart's repose,
after long wandering over the face of Earth,
vanquishing fear and temptation,
and contemplating in clarity the world,
in Self-reflection
has forged —:
Sound let it become,
as Word resound,
by the community borne,
to waken Mankind.

What did the Wanderer find
returning from heavenly realms
into Time's course?
— Homelessness on earth.

Peering from the high peak
he is filled with longing;
a huge hunger for redemption
hollows him,
and his eyes, imbibing the sky's
azure
looking inward
consume his heart.
He seeks out paths.
Human advice leads him astray.
The line of the horizon, full of promise, lies.
The outstretched rim covers the brim
of his coffin.
The Earth is the grave of Mankind.

In this deep darkness appeared the Master
and with light hand lifted the sombre lid.
The Wanderer sees in orderly design
Star on Star.
Conjoined with one another they became
a Head
with Arms extended toward him full of love
bearing him, when already life was fleeing
and his joints were loosening,
raising him upright in footprints,
which were hewn deep in the earth.
But the Wanderer knew:
These were footsteps of his Destiny,
pre-carved for him for times to come,
circumscribing the space which had to be paced.

O schaue!
Die Stapfen werden zu Stufen
und führen hinunter ins Erdeninnere.
Es läuft ein Gang durch viele Schichten.
Er schreitet schauend in tieferes Dunkel.
In völliger Nacht verkündet der Führer
das Werden der Welten, den Willen der Götter,
im grollenden Grunde,
im Brausen und Branden der Elemente.

Wo seine Worte ertönten,
da griffen Dämonen zu Schaufel und Hammer
und türmten die Tore zu einem Tempel.
Im Mittelpunkt der Erde aber glüht
der Plan des Himmels.
Und wie der Wandrer das Kreuz erblickt im Kreis,
den Säulengang gewölbt,
ist seine Schwere hingeschwunden.
Er steigt nach oben.
Steigen aber heisst das Haus errichten,
sagt der Meister und verleiht ihm Werkzeug.

Jetzt harrt er,
nach langer Arbeit
emporgereckt in hoher Halle,
vor einem Altar.
Der ist mit einem Tuch verhüllt,
ihm eingewoben sieht er einen Doppelbaum
aus rot und blauen Zweigen,
von einem Ton bewegt, der auf und nieder schwebt.
Da atmete der Wandrer leicht
und hob den Teppich weg
und fand den Kelch voll·Licht
und trank, —
und immer träufelte der Himmelstau herab.
Das waren Tropfen von den Sternen.

Und wiederum erblickt er, wie am Anfang,
ein Haupt
mit Armen, nach vorne voller Liebe ausgestreckt,
und hört des Engels Wort:
Erkenne dich als Wachender
im eignen Haus.
Der Leib des Menschen ist die Tat
der Götter.

O see!
The steps become stairs
and lead down into the center of the Earth.
Through many layers runs a passage.
He strides seeing into deeper darkness.
In pitch-black night his Guide proclaims
the World's evolution, the will of the Gods,
in the rumbling depth,
in the roaring and storming of the elements.

Where his words resounded,
there Demons took hold of shovel and hammer
erecting the towering gates to a Temple.
At the core of Earth, however, glows
the plan of Heaven.
And when the Wanderer discerns the Cross within the Sphere,
the vaulted colonnade,
his heavy oppressoin dwindles away.
He rises upwards.
Rising, however, means erecting the House,
says the Master, and lends him work-tools.

Now he bides
after long toil
upright in the tall hall,
before an Altar.
This is enveloped by a cloth,
inwoven he discerns a Double-tree,
with branches red and blue,
stirred by a tone, swaying up and down.
Light was the Wanderer's breath;
he lifted the tapestry
and found the Chalice filled with light
and drank, —
and ever trickled down the heavenly Dew.
Those were dew-drops from the stars.

And once again he sees as at the start,
a Head
with Arms, extended toward him full of love,
and hears the Angel's word:
Know thyself as one awakened
in thine own House.
The Body of Man is the Deed
of the Gods.

In die Leere des Hauptes . . .

In die Leere des Hauptes,
das nicht mehr Gedanken empfängt,
im Alpdruck der Brust,
der den Atem erstickt,
in der Ohnmacht der Glieder,
die keine Kraft zu gehen erringen,
— ach, in der Last des ganzen Leibes,
den nimmer die Quellen des irdischen Lebens
zu erfrischen vermögen —:
Hält mich nur aufrecht
die Knochengestalt meines Körpers.
Aber durch die redet der Tod:
     Ja!
Du hast die Stufe erstiegen,
wo die Weltenseele gekreuzigt wird!
— Und ich sehe das Kreuz
wachsen am Erdenrand,
da die Sonne gesunken.
Es richtet sich auf
in die Höhe des Himmels.
O Todes-Merkmal!
Aber die Sterne umkreisen die Achse des Kreuzes
und tönen:
Christus ist vom Tode auferstanden!

In die Leere des Hauptes . . .

In the void of the head,
that no more thoughts conceives,
in the nightmare of the chest,
that strangles the breath,
in the weakness of the limbs
that can muster no strength to walk,
O, in the weariness of the whole body,
that no more the springs of earthly life
will ever refresh —:
Only my body's
skeleton form holds me upright.
Through it, however, speaks to me Death:
    Yes!
You have ascended the steps
where the World-soul is crucified!
— And I see the Cross
growing on the earth-rim,
as the sun has set.
It raises itself
in the heights of heaven,
O sign of Death!
But the stars revolve around the Axis of the Cross
and intone:
Christ has risen from death!

Allein gelassen . . .

Allein gelassen
in dieser Öde,
der alle entfliehen,
die den nur erfasst, der verharrt,
jedoch, in der auch der helfende Weltgeist
sich naht,
zu suchen ein Herz,
das Heimat ihm gibt.
Und findet er keines,
so fällt ins Nichtsein
die Allheit
hienieden.

Einsam,
die anderen träumen am Mondsee, der unrein geworden,
Fische, tot an den Strand geschwemmt.
Aber wer spürt noch den Verwesungsgeruch?
Es bräunt in sengender Sonne das Menschengeschlecht
die gottentfremdeten Glieder.
Schlamm wühlt empor.
Faune der Tiefe macht es zu Satyrn und Nixen.
Alle vergassen den Abfall vom Engel.
Geistentseeltes Getobe, betäubendes Lustgeschrei
in der Schwüle brütender Lüfte.
Tierheit, vom Sonnendämon gelockt,
lugt aus dem Abgrund.

Ichheit, wach' und erwecke!
Hinab in die Nacht der wiederkehrenden Rassen
streue der Sternkleinodien
heilsame Geistsaat
auf die vergiftete Erde.

Allein gelassen . . .

Left alone
in this wasteland,
from which all flee,
which seizes him only who stays,
yet in which also the helping Spirit
draws near,
to seek a heart,
that will offer him homeland.
And if he finds none,
into the void, then,
falls the All
here below.

Lonesome,
the others dream by the moon-lake, grown impure.
Dead fish, washed ashore on the beach.
But who still senses the stench of decay?
In the parching sun the human race is tanning
the god-estranged limbs.
Mud wallows to the surface.
Fauns of the deep it transforms to satyrs and nixies.
All have forgotten their fall from the Angel.
Ravings, spirit-devoid, deafening screams of lust,
in the sultry brooding air.
Bestiality, enticed by the Sun-demon,
peeks from the abyss.

Selfhood, awake and awaken!
Down to the night of re-emerging races
strew the star-gems
wholesome Spirit-seed
upon the poisoned earth.

Abendgang

Betrunkner Greis in der Gasse.
Am Waldrand beim Wohnwagen Mord.
Vom Irrenhaus her Gewitter-kündendes Toben.
Sonatenklänge aus der Mansarde verweht.
Umnachteter Musiker weint.
Mutter, die ihren Säugling im Bade erwürgt hat.
Über die Selbstmörderbrücke
bei der Verbrecherspelunke vorbei.
Am Kiosk die Zeitung durchblättert:
Radioaktiver Staub in den Wolken,
Zugvogelschar, die tot zur Erde gefallen,
Tiefseefische, verwest an den Strand getrieben . . .
"Guten Abend, Professor, wie geht's?"
"Müde, ich operiere am laufenden Band im Spital.
Kein Mensch, der genest, wird besser durch mich.
Baldigst Ferien wäre alleiniger Lichtblick.
Aber die Menschheit ist krank."
Elend eines Tages wie vieler.
Und du willst es verwandeln mit Worten?
Niemand vernimmt dich.
Darfst du klagen darüber?
Was könnte Klage bedeuten,
gemessen am Leiden, ach, des Erlösers?

Abendgang
Evening Stroll

Drunken old man in the alley.
On the wood's edge near the caravan, murder.
From the madhouse, ravings presaging storm.
Sonata-sounds, drifting away from the attic.
Maddened musician moans.
Mother, who strangled her infant in the bath.
Over the suicide bridge
past the nearby criminals' tavern.
At the kiosk perusing the newspapers:
Radioactive dust in the clouds,
a swarm of migrating birds, fallen dead to the earth,
deep-sea fish, driven rotting ashore . . .
"Good evening, Professor, how goes it?"
"Tired, from performing operations on an assembly line.
No man who recovers, is improved by me.
Holidays soon would be my only bright spot.
But Mankind is sick."
Misery one day like the rest.
And you wish to transform it with words?
No one listens to you.
Dare you complain?
What is the good of complaining,
measured against the pain, ah, of the Redeemer?

Das Ich, im Leib verhaftet, todbewusst ...

Das Ich, im Leib verhaftet, todbewusst,
holt von der Sonne sich Unsterblichkeit.
Des Körpers Sterben zahlt es als Tribut,
Verwesung dehnt sich über alle Welt.

O Blume, Biene, Vogel, Schmetterling,
des Lichtes Kinder, die durch meine Lust
nach Ewigkeit dem Nichts ich übergab,
wie kann ich als Unsterblicher bestehn?

Es hebt der Sonnensohn sich aus dem Grab.
Er trägt an seinem Auferstehungsleib
die Wunden, die das Ich der Schöpfung schlug,
geheilt als Sternenschrift, die Tröstung strahlt.

Das Ich, im Leib verhaftet, todbewusst ...

The 'I', a body-captive, death-aware,
draws from the Sun its immortality.
The body's dying pays it as tribute;
corruption spreads out over all the world.

O bee and blossom, bird and butterfly,
children of light, whom I have through my lust
for eternal life, surrendered to the void,
how may I as immortal stand the test?

The Solar Son arises from the grave.
He bears upon His resurrected Body
the wounds, that Ego to creation smote,
healed as a star script, raying consolation.

Wie das Ich den Körper verlassen . . .

Wie das Ich den Körper verlassen,
fährt es im Mond-Schiff auf den Wogen des Weltmeers.
Wellen, veilchenfarben, tragen es ostwärts,
und der Wille verleiht ihm Segel
— Fittiche sind es von Adlern —.
Wasser wird Wolke, weisses Gebild im Azur,
überweht von der Trikolore der Luft,
blauende Andacht, grünende Hoffnung, purpurne Liebe.
Und es entfaltet sich im Gezelt ein goldenes Dreieck.
Helios selber tritt nun hervor.
Den Gestorbenen hebt er an das unsterbliche Herz,
schenkt ihm das Auge des Äons.

Auf die Erde schaut der Tote zurück,
durch Sphären, Farben und Fluten,
die jetzt veratmen, verlöschen, versiegen,
bis auf den eigenen Körper,
sieht ihn der Erde vereint.
Er hat die Spuren der Krankheit,
die Runen des Todes,
den Hauch der Verwesung verloren.
Äther ist er geworden,
weil Christus heiligt jedes Atom.

Der Raum, den der Tote verlassen,
ist wie die Wabe aus Wachs,
von heiligen Bienen gebaut,
glänzend gleich dem Kristall.
Und das ewige Ich blickt hinein in das leere Gehäuse,
wissend, es ist die Wiege des schuldlos werdenden Wesens,
das wieder heimkehrt vom Himmel,
um Mensch zu werden auf Erden,
vorbestimmtes Endziel am Anfang der Schöpfung,
eh noch gewesen Gestirne, Sonne und Mond:
Ur-Sein, geborgen im Wort.

Mein Ich darf wohnen darin,
wie jedes und alle, im eignen Gemach,
vor ihm Geborene, nach ihm Gestorbene,
sicher der Einkehr und Heimstatt,
zusammen mit seinen Gefährten, ·
in Freiheit und Liebe erwählt.

Siehst du die Waben
von Engeln behütet?
Da ist kein Sterbebett mehr,
nur Sternengelasse.

Wie das Ich den Körper verlassen . . .

As the 'I' abandons the body,
it sails in the Moon-ship on the waves of the Cosmic Sea.
Billows, violet-hued, bear it eastward,
and the will lends it sails
— Wings are they of eagles —.
Water is cloud now, white form in the azure,
over it wafts, three-colored banner, the air,
blueing devotion, green-growing hope, deep-purple love.
In heaven's tent unfolds a golden triangle.
Helios himself now appears.
He raises the Departed to the immortal Heart,
grants him the Eye of the Aeon.

Back to the earth gazes he who has died,
through spheres, colors and floods,
which now expire, fade, and dissolve,
unto his own body;
he sees it joined to the earth.
He has lost the traces of illness,
the runes of death,
the breath of decay.
Ether has he become,
for Christ hallows every atom.
The room, the dead has abandoned,
is like the honeycomb,
built by the sacred bees,
gleaming even as crystal.
And the immortal 'I' gazes into the empty husk,
knowing, it is the cradle of the being becoming pure,
returning home from heaven,
to become Man on earth,
pre-ordained destination from the dawn of creation,
even before stars, sun and moon existed:
Primordial-being, sheltered in the Word.

My 'I' may live therein,
as each and all, in their own chamber,
before him born, after him dead,
certain of refuge and homestead,
together with his companions,
chosen in freedom and love.

Do you behold the honeycombs
guarded by Angels?
No death-bed is here,
only cells of stars.

47

Zeitgedichte

(Friedrich Hiebel zum sechzichsten Geburtstag)

I

Wer vermöchte,
durch des Körpers Beschwerden
mit Schwermut belastet,
den Lebenden jetzt noch zu helfen?
Es schwindet sein Ich in der Ohnmacht dahin.
Aber wohin?
— Zu den Toten.
Die ihr unsterblich geworden, so sinnt er, wo bleibt ihr?
Bin ich euch völlig entfremdet?
Habt ihr euch nichts von der Erde,
das tröstlich wäre, bewahrt?
Nicht mehr die Wärme des Herzens,
des Odems Kühle nicht mehr?
Und sie sagen:
Noch lebt das Gelöbnis des Geistes im Wort,
sendet in die geläuterte Seele Liebe und Licht,
die das Weltall durchwallen.
Wir erfahren ihr Wesen,
weil wir im Reigen der Wandelgestirne
den Urgesang der Schöpfung geschritten.
Die Töne verleihen uns dann die himmlische Ichheit,
wenn das irdische Ich abfällt vom Knochengerüst,
wie die Schneelast sich löst von dem Felsen
und als Lawine zur Tiefe hinabstürzt,
vereist auf schwarzer Moräne.
Aber die Eiskristalle verkünden den Sechsstrahl der Sterne,
wonach der Tempel des Körpers gebaut ist.
Darunter keimen die Blumen und weisen zum Urselbst.

Zeitgedichte
Period Poems

I

Who, burdened with melancholy,
through an ailing body,
is still able to help the living?
His 'I' swoons away in a faint.
But where to
— To the Dead.
You who have grown immortal, he muses, where are you?
Am I wholly estranged from you?
Did you preserve from the earth
nothing which might console?
No more the warmth of the heart,
the cool of the breath no more?
And they say:
The vow of the Spirit still lives in the Word;
into the purified soul, it sends love and light,
which surge through the Cosmos.
We experience their essence,
for in the round of the planets,
the primal Song of Creation we paced.
The tones then bestow on us the heavenly Selfhood,
when the earthly 'I' falls from the bony structure,
as the weight of snow from the rock
plunges as avalanche into the depths,
frozen on the black moraine.
But the ice-crystals proclaim the stars' sixfold ray,
forming the basis of the body's temple.
Below germinate flowers and point to the Primal Self.

Furchtbar ist die Versuchung, zu verfallen dem Schein,
dass des Satans Tod-verleihende Schwere
senke sich auf das göttliche Schöpferwort,
übergebe die Seele dem Grauen.
Alle heilig-hehren Namen,
lichtlos dem Himmel entgleitend,
Steine, Pflanzen und Tiere —
nichts als Abfall!
Der Raum, das All in sich tragend,
sonnendurchwirktes Farbengewebe,
Laute der Sterne,
Töne, vom Donner gezeugt,
lassen nur Leere zurück.
Die Zeit, die Wesen entlassend,
welche am Weltbau geschaffen,
rollt in sich selber zurück.
Freunde, jahrtausendelang
vom Schicksal geschlagen,
werden zerstreut.
Schaffende Jünger der Ältern,
die noch die Götter erschauten,
haben versagt.
Seit sie den Stachel des bösen Geredes gebrauchten,
klingt von den Lippen hohl das Gebet,
das früher die Leidenden heilte.
Ach, es bleibt jetzt nur eines: lauschen, bis die Gestorbnen
selber verkünden das Wort,
wie im Äther es west
also unsterbliche Dichtung.

II

Fearful is the temptation, to fall prey to the semblance,
that Satan's death-bestowing weight
may sink onto the Divine Creative Word,
surrender the soul to horror.
All the holy noble names,
lightless, slide out of heaven;
stones, plants, animals —
nothing but waste!
Space, bearing within it the All,
sun-enwoven web of colors,
sounds of stars,
tones, by thunder engendered,
leave behind them but void.
Time releasing the beings,
who worked on the Cosmic Building,
rolls back into itself.
Friends, for millenia
beaten by destiny
are scattered.
Creative disciples of the Elders,
who still beheld the Gods,
have failed.
Since they used the sting of the gossip of evil,
hollow sounds the prayer from their lips,
where once it healed the suffering.
Alas, but one thing remains: to listen until the Departed
themselves proclaim the Word,
as it holds sway in the ether
as an immortal Poem.

Schon in Erdbereichen erwachet!
Schaut eure Lebensgefährten, die durch das Sterben gegangen,
auferstanden im Geist,
die himmlischen Sphären erwandernd.
Herrlich waren die Reisen hienieden,
herrlicher aber sollen sie werden im Himmel.
Siehe den strahlenden Führer,
von den Sternen gesandt,
uns zu versammeln,
den heiligen Seraph,
der uns von Westen nach Osten geleitet,
über die Berge und Meere,
das Menschheits-Ich zu verkünden
den Völkern
und aufzuerwecken die Toten,
die liegen in Särgen
gebannt an die Leiber.
Und es ersetzt ihnen Satan
die verwesenden Glieder mit toten Substanzen.
"Dies ist die Strafe", so spricht der Ungeist,
"für ihre Verbrechen."
Aber es wird die Rinde der Erde zerfetzt von den Bomben
der rächenden Sekte,
und die Seelen, befreit von dem Körper,
ertrinken in Bächen von Tränen,
die in den Acheron stürzen.
Ach, auch der schrecklichste Scherge
ersehnt die Sühne,
gutzumachen die Untat.
Und wir wollen den Funken der Liebe,
den der Sohn als Versöhner
in die Ichheit gelegt,
nie mehr erlöschen lassen,
selbst in den Tiefen des Ozeans nicht,
unter den Faunen und Satyrn.
Seraph des Lichtes, hilf uns,
zu verwandeln die Bosheit.
Führ uns auf die heiligen Berge
himmlischer Läuterung.
Ihr, die ihr noch im Erdenleibe verweilet,
schliesst euch der Schar der Unsterblichen an.

III

Awake, even in earthly realms!
Behold your life-companions who have passed through death,
resurrected in spirit,
wandering through heavenly spheres.
Glorious were the journeys on earth,
more glorious still shall they be in Heaven.
See the radiant Guide,
sent from the stars,
to assemble us;
the holy Seraph,
who led us from West to East,
over the mountains and seas,
to proclaim the Ego of Man
to the peoples
and to awaken the Dead,
who are lying in coffins
bound to their bodies.
And Satan exchanges for them
decaying limbs with lifeless substance.
"This is retribution," so speaks the non-Spirit,
"for their criminal deeds."
But the crust of Earth is rent by bombs
of the avenging sect,
and the souls, freed from the body,
drown in rivers of tears,
which plunge into the Acheron.
Ah, even the most fearsome henchman
longs for atonement,
to right the crime.
And we will allow the spark of love,
which the Son as Mediator
laid in the Selfhood,
nevermore to be quenched
not even in the depths of the ocean,
among fauns and satyrs.
Seraph of Light, help us,
to transform malice.
Lead us to the hallowed hills
of heavenly purification.
You, who still in Earth-form dwell,
join the ranks of the Immortals.

Schlacke des Mondes, der vor die Sonne getreten ...

Schlacke des Mondes, der vor die Sonne getreten,
so dass Finsternis sich verbreitet hienieden,
durch die toten Gedanken Leben vernichtend.

In dem Schatten ersterben Pflanzen und Tiere.
Tötende Triebe erwachen in den Geschlechtern.
Nur der Tod erschliesst dem Lichte die Tore.

Doch es tritt mit ausgebreiteten Armen
durch die Balken des Kreuzes, als Tao errichtet,
Helios selber, im Menschenherzen zu wohnen.

— *So* erblicken die Toten, die schauend geworden,
durch die Tat des Auferstandnen die Erde,
die sie verliessen, webend im Werden der Welten.

Schlacke des Mondes, der vor die Sonne getreten

Slag of the moon, moving in front of the sun,
so that darkness is spreading here below,
through the deadened thoughts destroying life.

In the shadow expire plant and beast.
Murderous instincts awaken in the people.
Death alone opens the gates to Light.

But there appears with widely outstretched arms
through the beams of the Cross, erected as TAO,
Helios himself, to dwell in the heart of Man.

— So the Dead, who have become seers, behold
through the deed of the Resurrected, the earth
they have abandoned, weaving in worlds evolving.

Staatsbegräbnis

Sieh dich aufmerksam um, was auf der Erde geschieht—
Da steigen gescheite, gediegne, gesittete Männer,
sich gegenseitig gefällig, in ein gemeinsames Flugzeug,
um über das Weltmeer zu fahren,
dort dem grossen Staatsmann das Totengeleite zu geben.
Pakete, nicht zu vergessen, in Seitentaschen:
Friedensvorschläge.
Doch sie zu zitieren, ist jetzt nicht die Zeit.
Sie essen ein bisschen, sie rauchen ein bisschen,
sie dösen ein bisschen.
Sie denken (denken sie wirklich?): da oben im Weltall kommt
gar nichts heraus.

— Die Sonne geht unter,
jetzt schlafen sie ein.
Von dem, was drüben der Tote erlebt, weiss keiner etwas,
oder er sagt es doch nicht.
Und das ist noch schlimmer.
Wie sich aus dem westlichen Erdteil elektrische Blitze erheben,
im östlichen blaue Dünste gespensterhaft hinziehen,
nichts erblicken die Schläfer von der himmlischen Stadt,
vor deren Toren der Tote nun steht.
Nichts von den Pfeilern der Weisheit und Liebe,
nichts von den Architraven des Schicksals,
nichts von den Fresken der Völkerseelen
im Kreuzgewölbe des Menscheitsbaues,
nichts von der Gutmachung der Missetaten,
nichts von dem Ziele der Erde,
nichts, aber gar nichts davon,
dass der Mensch-gewordene Gott für alle gestorben.

— Und dann erwachen sie wieder, greifen nach ihren Akten,
steigen aus,
sagen nichts mit vielen Worten,
sitzen, dinieren und schreiten Ehrengeleite ab,
hören Nekrologe und Gebete.
— Aber was ihr Kollege, der Tote, drüben erlebt,
das ist belanglos für sie.
Niemand sagt etwas, das seine Taten auf Erden
im Himmel fortsetzen könnte.
Und er selber kann sie, die Nichtse, auch nicht erreichen.
— Was soll man darüber nun denken?
Hilflos sind sie,
die gescheiten, gediegnen, gesitteten Leute,
die das Geschick der Menschheit leiten.
Aber der Erkennenden kämpfen umsonst
Jahrzehnt um Jahrzehnt.
— Man hört nur die Nichtssagenden.

Staatsbegräbnis
State Funeral

Note carefully events upon the Earth —
Sophisticated, stolid citizens, congenial
gentlemen, board a special airplane,
to journey across the World-ocean,
to pay their last respects to the Great Statesman.
Important documents in attache cases:
Peace proposals.
But to cite them is clearly not the moment.
They eat a bit, they smoke a bit,
they doze a bit.
They think (do they really think?): Up there in the Cosmos
nothing transpires.

— The sun sets;
now they fall asleep.
What the dead is experiencing there beyond, none knows,
or else, none speaks of it:
Which is even worse.
As in the western continent, electrical storms gather,
and in the East, blue mists, phantom-like, trail,
naught perceive the sleepers, of the Heavenly City,
before whose gates the dead now stands.
Naught of the pillars of wisdom and love,
naught of Destiny's architraves,
naught of the frescoes of the folk-souls,
in the cross-vaults of the Building of Man,
naught of the atonement for sinful deeds,
naught of the goals of the Earth,
nothing, but absolutely nothing of Him,
the God, made Man, who died for us all.

— And then they wake up again, grope for their cases,
stagger out,
speak much but say nothing,
sit, dine, and stride as an Honor Guard,
hear funeral orations and prayers.
— But what their colleague, the dead, is experiencing beyond,
that is irrelevant.
No one says anything that might continue
his earthly deeds in heaven.
And neither is he himself, able to reach these naughts.
— What should one make of this?
Helpless are they,
these sophisticated, solid and well-bred gentlemen
who guide the fate of Mankind.
Decade after decade,
the conscious ones struggle in vain.
— One hears only the naught-sayers.

Der Tote sagt:

Mein Ich ist ein Sendling
aus den Seraphischen Sphären
und soll auf der Erde,
wo du noch verweilst,
dich behüten.
Es schaut dich umgeben
von Sinnesfarben,
worin die Sonne erloschen:

Gelb, das vergilbt, und Blau, das verblasst.
Graues Gespinst verdämmert im finsteren Raum.
Rot, es tropft auf die Blache das Blut.
Aber den Teppich erlittner Verbrechen schleppen auch Tote:
Einverwoben ist Marter und Mord,
Mitleid, hilflos geworden.
Sieh mein ewiges Ich, das von den Gestirnen erstrahlt,
es entknüpft die Knäuel des Schicksals,
löst im Lichte die Naht und Not der dunklen Gewalten,
und die Fäden erglänzen als das Gefieder des Phönix.
Komm, entfliege dem Grab . . .

Der Tote sagt:
The Dead speaks:

My 'I' is a herald
from the Seraphim's sphere,
and its task on earth,
where you still dwell ,
is to guard you.
It sees you surrounded
by senses' colors,
wherein the Sun is effaced:

Yellow, that sallows, and blue, that pales,
Grey webs fade to dusk in the darkening room.
Red, the blood drops on the shroud.
But also the Dead drag the tapestry of suffered crimes:
Interwoven are torture and murder,
compassion, grown helpless.
See my immortal 'I', which from the stars rays forth,
it unties the knots of Fate,
loosens in light the seams and sores of the powers of darkness,
and the glistening threads are the plumage of the Phoenix.
Come, fly from the grave . . .

Schwermut will sinnen in mir . . .

Schwermut will sinnen in mir,
wie alles Erinnern verblasst,
sich verlierend im Nichts.
Füsse, die über die Erde geschritten,
erkalten.
Ach, der Körper, von Adam, aus dem Grabe
versetzt,
bringt den Tod in das Weltall,
und der Stoff muss verstieben.

Aber da tropft von den Balken
das Blut zum Boden herunter,
Purpurn, vom Lichte durchstrahlt
als leuchtender Tau,
der das Erdreich durchsickert,
erstrahlt als Gestein.

Schwermut will sinnen in mir . . .

Sad mood will make me ponder,
how all remembrance fades,
vanishing into the void.
Feet, which wandered over the earth,
grow cold.
Ah, the body of Adam, out of the grave
transplaced,
brings to the Universe death,
and substance must turn to dust.

But there drops from the rafters
the Blood down to the ground.
Purple, with light trans-rayed,
as luminous dew,
which trans-pierces the earth,
radiates as stone.

Was für ein furchtbarer, dreimal erdröhnender Wehruf . . .

Was für ein furchtbarer, dreimal erdröhnender Wehruf
überwältigt dein Ich,
schreckt es ins Nichts zurück?
Dein volles zum Himmel erhobenes Auge
wird hohl vor Entsetzen:
Versiegt der kristallene Quell,
das göttliche Feuer erloschen,
entfärbt alle Farben der irdischen Reiche
und die geliebten Gesichter der Menschen so fahl!
Die Welt im Schatten,
und, ihm zu entfliehen,
erwacht unmenschliche Gier,
die alles, um sich zu erhalten, verschlingt,
und Angst zugleich, dass die Nahrung
zum Gift wird.
Krankheit ergreift deinen Körper,
alles führt nur zum Tode.
Bin ich es noch, so fragst du,
oder gehört der Hass in den zerfallenden Knochen,
die Hitze im Blute
dem ganzen Menschengeschlechte,
das bös ist —
ach, erweist sich die Menschheit
zum Morde bestimmt?
Das sagen alle Verbrechen auf Erden,
im Buche des Weltalls verzeichnet.
Mitverschuldet ist jeder
am Martergerichte
der Völker.
Wie aber werden die Toten
empfangen die Lebenden drüben?
In Abscheu wenden sie sich
selbst von den Liebsten auf Erden hinweg.
Aber, o Wunder,
sie sehen nur einen einzigen Leib
mit Wunden bedeckt, aber vernarbt.
Die Narben leuchten als Sterne,
die Hände halten die Chronik des Todes empor.
Leer sind die Seiten
im Buche des Lebens.

Was für ein furchtbarer, dreimal erdröhnender Wehruf . . .

What a fearful, thrice-wailed cry of woe
overwhelms your Self,
frightens it back to the void?
Your wide-open eye uplifted to heaven
hollows with horror:
Parched the crystalline spring,
the divine fire extinguished,
faded all colors of the earthly realm
and the dear faces of men so ashen!
The world in shadow,
and, to flee it,
excites inhuman greed,
which devours all to sustain itself,
along with fear, that the food
turns to poison.
Sickness lays hold of your body,
all leads but to death.
Am I still I, you ask,
or is hatred in the crumbling bones,
heat in the blood
linked to all humankind,
which is evil —
Ah, does mankind confirm itself
destined to murder?
So say all crimes on the earth,
inscribed in the Book of the Cosmos.
Co-partners in guilt are all
in the torture trial
of nations.
How will the Dead, however,
receive the living yonder?
In horror they turn away
even from the dearest on earth.
But, O wonder,
they behold only the one body
with wounds bedecked, but scarred.
The scars shine like stars,
the hands hold the Chronicle of Death on high.
Blank are the pages
in the Book of Life.

Der Auferstandene sagt:
O Lebender, nimm das Blut,
das wie die Rosenblüte so rein ist,
das Wasser der Träne, geheiligtes Salz,
und ausgelöscht
sind so im Buche des Lebens
die Seiten, wo einst
deine Untaten standen,
aufgehoben im Worte,
dessen Laute als Sterne
am Dom des Gottes
erglänzen.

Freue dich, Mensch, an den
Blumen der Erde,
am Lächeln der Kinder,
in der Gemeinschaft
deiner Geschwister im Geiste.
Alle Engel lieben dich
wieder.
Es ist das Opfer des Christus,
das dich erlöst.
Als Erlösten erkennen wir
dich
auf dem wiedererstandenen
Sterne.
Beginne
begeistert —

The Risen One speaks:
O living one, take the blood,
that is pure as blossoms of roses,
the water of tears, sanctified salt;
effaced are thus
in the book of life, the pages
where once
your misdeeds were inscribed,
sheltered in the Word
whose sounds as stars
on the Dome of God
ray forth.

Take joy, O Man, in the
blossoms of earth,
in smiles of the children,
in communion
with your brothers in the Spirit
All the Angels love you
once more.
It is the Offering of Christ,
that redeems you.
As redeemed, we know
you
on the new-risen
Star.
Begin
inspired —

Winde, / was ihr weht, / ist Weh.

Winde,
was ihr weht,
ist Weh.

Donner,
was ihr rollt,
ist Rache.

Tränen,
was ihr tropft,
ist Tod.

Boden,
was du birgst,
sind Blumen.

Winde, / was ihr weht, / ist Weh.

Winds,
what you whine,
is woe.

Thunders,
what you roll,
is vengeance.

Tears,
what you drop,
is death.

Soil,
what you shelter
are blossoms.

Works by Albert Steffen

Novels:

Ott, Alois and Werelsche. 1907.
Die Bestimmung der Roheit. 1912.
Die Erneuerung des Bundes. 1913.
Der rechte Liebhaber des Schicksals. 1916.
Sibylla Mariana. 1917.
Lebensgeschichte eines jungen Menschen. 1928.
Wildeisen. 1929.
Sucher nach sich selbst. 1931.
Aus Georg Archibalds Lebenslauf und nachgelassenen
    Schriften. 1950.
Oase der Menschlichkeit. 1954.
Altmanns Memoiren aus dem Krankenhaus. 1956.
Dreiunddreissig Jahre. 1959.
Die Mission der Poesie. 1962.

Elisabeth Steffen / Selbstgewähltes Schicksal
    Mit Gedenkworten von Albert Steffen. 1961.

Remembrances. sketches and miniatures

Kleine Mythen. 1923.
Pilgerfahrt zum Lebensbaum. 1925.
In Memoriam Rudolf Steiner. 1925.
Lebenswende. 1931.
Merkbuch. 1937.
Buch der Rückschau. 1938.
Selbsterkenntnis und Lebenschau. 1940.
Auf Geisteswegen. 1942.
Der Genius des Todes. 1943.
Novellen. 1947.
Aus der Mappe eines Geistsuchers. 1951.
Gedenkbilder für Elisabeth Steffen. Mit zwölf farbigen
    Aquarellwiedergaben. 1961.
Lebensbilder an der Todespforte. Mit zwölf farbigen
    Aquarellwiedergaben. 1963.
Reisen hüben und drüben. Mit vierzehn farbig wieder-
    gegebenen Skizzen. 1963.

Poems

Wegzehrung. 1921.
Gedichte. 1931.
Der Tröster. 1935.
Passiflora / Ein Requiem für Felicitas. 1939.
Wach auf, du Todesschläfer. 1941.
Epoche. 1944.
Spätsaat. 1947.
Am Kreuzweg des Schicksals. 1952.
Krankheit nicht zum Tode. 1955.
Steig auf den Parnass und schaue. 1960.
Im Sterben auferstehen. 1964.

Dramas

Der Auszug aus Ägypten / Die Manichäer. 1916.
Das Viergetier. 1920.
Hieram und Salomo. 1925.
Der Chef des Generalstabs. 1927.
Der Sturz des Antichrist. 1928.
Das Todeserlebnis des Manes. 1934.
Adonis-Spiel / Eine Herbstesfeier. 1935.
Friedenstragödie. 1936.
Fahrt ins andere Land. 1938.
Pestalozzi. 1939.
Märtyrer. 1942.
Ruf am Abgrund. 1943.
Karoline von Günderrode. 1946.
Barrabas. 1949.
Alexanders Wandlung. 1953.
Lin. 1957.

Essays

Begegnungen mit Rudolf Steiner. 1926/1955.
Mani / Sein Leben und seine Lehre. 1930.
Goethes Geistgestalt. 1932.
Conrad Ferdinand Meyers lebendige Gestalt. 1937.
Lebensbildnis Pestalozzis. 1939.
Die Krisis im Leben des Künstlers. 1922.
Der Künstler zwischen Westen und Osten. 1925.
Der Künstler und die Erfüllung der Mysterien. 1928.
Dramaturgische Beiträge zu den Schönen Wissenschaften. 1935.
Frührot der Mysteriendichtung. 1940.
Geistige Heimat. 1941.
Krisis, Katharsis, Therapie im Geistesleben der
    Gegenwart. 1944.
Vorhut des Geistes. 1945.
Wiedergeburt der Schönen Wissenschaften. 1946.
Mysterienflug. 1948.
Geist-Erkenntnis / Gottes-Liebe. 1949.
Dichtung als Weg zur Einweihung. 1960.
Brennende Probleme. 1956.

ALBERT STEFFEN

World literary judgment may well consider Albert Steffen, distinguished Swiss poet, dramatist, novelist and essayist, as one of the greatest literary figures of the twentieth century.

He was born in 1884 and died on July 15, 1963, the author of over seventy volumes of published works, few of which have been translated into English. Thus, the present volume, SELECTED POEMS OF ALBERT STEFFEN, translated by the American poet, *Daisy Aldan,* whose only authorized translation of Stephane Mallarme's UN COUP DE DES, (called by Gide, "The most untranslatable poem in any language,") was widely praised, will be welcomed by the English speaking world.

". . . There is no moral narrowness, no sitting in judgment, no lack of understanding in the poet's view. Life is to him not a mere spectacle of nature, but rather eternal doing, struggling and suffering of that highest faculty of love in the conquest and meaningfulness of which he believes.

Hermann Hesse

"After reading Albert Steffen's books, one feels cleaner and better and this effect alone is so rare in the work of a writer and poet, that it gives to it a special significance."

Dr. Robert Faesi — (Hon. Prof. — Univ. for Modern German Lit., Zurich)

". . . His words play in a convincing way between the spheres of spirit and of the senses, so that we may experience this poet as thoroughly modern, but in addition — and this distinguishes him from many others — true and genuine in every fiber."

Dr. Walter Muschg — (author of "Von Trakl Zu Brecht")

ABOUT THE TRANSLATOR

DAISY ALDAN

Daisy Aldan is the author of three volumes of Poetry: *The Destruction of Cathedrals*, (Two Cities Press), *Seven: Seven, Poems and Photographs*, (Folder Editions), and *The Masks Are Becoming Faces*, (Goosetree Press). She is the Editor of *A New Folder: Americans: Poems and Drawings* (Folder Editions), and *Poems of India*, (Thomas Crowell, Pub.)

Awarded the 1967 DeWitt American Lyric Poetry award, her poems have appeared widely throughout the world. Her translations of Mallarme, Tzara, Breton, Rimbaud, Baudelaire, DeNerval, and many contemporary French and Spanish poets, are widely known.

While studying at the Goetheanum in Switzerland, she was introduced to the works of Albert Steffen by Ili Hackländer, with whom she collaborated to produce this volume.

Her translation with Elly Havas Simons of Albert Steffen's five act drama in blank verse, *The Death Experience of Manes*, will be published shortly.

Selected Poems of Albert Steffen has been printed
by The Pierson Press, New York, in Garamond
Type on Eagle A Text Laid paper. A limited number of copies has been bound in cloth.